# The Smells in God's World

**KATHRYN LUTZ**

Edited by
Patricia H. Lemon

Illustrated By
**Justin Wager**

**Graded Press**

NASHVILLE

Copyright © 1986 by Kathryn Lutz
Art copyright © 1986 by Graded Press
All rights reserved.
ISBN 0-939697-01-7
Manufactured in the United States of America

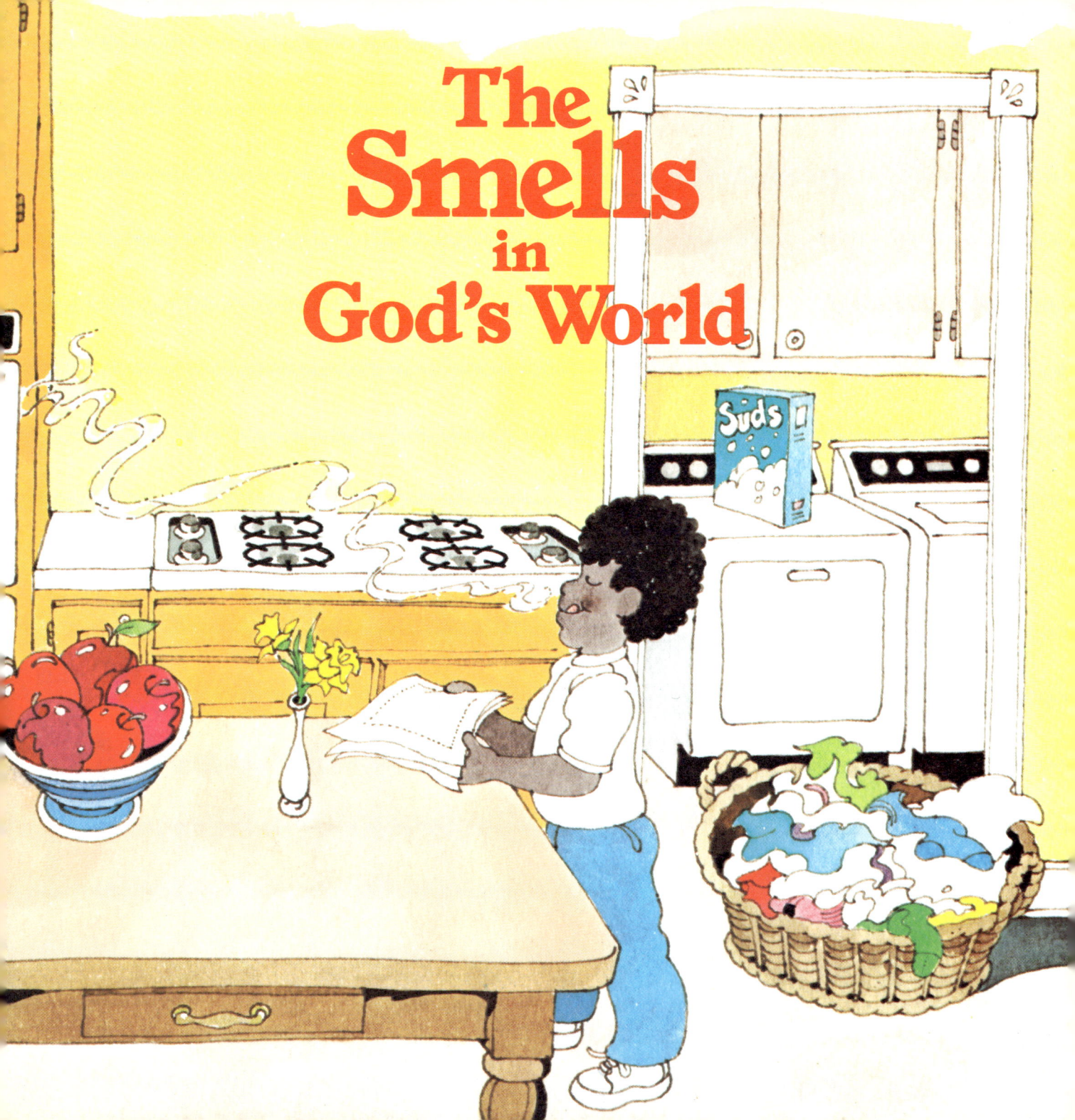

Robert played all morning with his trucks. His hands were dirty; his arms were dirty; his face was dirty. "Robert, it's lunch time," his mother called. Robert hurried inside to wash. He had soap bubbles all over his face. "Hmmmm," he said as he smelled the clean smell of soap.

God made my nose so I can tell
What things are by the smell.

I smell soap!
I can tell
By the smell.

"May I help you make lunch?" asked Robert. "I would love some help!" said his mother. "You could make us peanut butter sandwiches." Robert got the peanut butter and bread from the cabinet. He spread the peanut butter on each slice of bread. "Hmmmm," he said as he smelled the peanut butter.

God made my nose so I can tell
What things are by the smell.

I smell peanut butter!
I can tell
By the smell.

"Let's make some popcorn for dessert," suggested Robert's mother. "That's a great idea," said Robert. Together they poured the popcorn into the popcorn popper. "Hmmmm," said Robert as the kitchen filled with the smell of popcorn.

God made my nose so I can tell
What things are by the smell.

I smell popcorn!
I can tell
By the smell.

"Now I'm thirsty," said Robert. He got a tall glass of cold water. "I bet Daddy is thirsty, too," said Mother. "He's outside painting chairs." Robert hurried outside with a glass of cold water. "Thank you for the drink. I sure was thirsty," Daddy said as he handed Robert his empty glass. "Ooooh," Robert said as he walked back to the house. Paint was not his favorite smell.

God made my nose so I can tell
What things are by the smell.

I smell paint!
I can tell
By the smell.

Robert put the empty glass into the kitchen sink. "Robert, would you please take out the garbage?" asked his mother. "Sure," Robert replied. Mother handed him the garbage bag and opened the door. Robert opened the garbage can and dumped in the garbage. "Ooooh!" He quickly put the lid back on the can. The garbage smelled stinky!

God made my nose so I can tell
What things are by the smell.

I smell garbage!
I can tell
By the smell.

"What pretty flowers," thought Robert. "I bet Mom would like some for the kitchen table." He gently picked a flower. "Hmmmm," he said, "this flower smells sweet."

God made my nose so I can tell
What things are by the smell.

I smell flowers!
I can tell
By the smell.

"It's nearly dinner time, Robert. Would you help me set the table?" asked his mother. Robert got the napkins for the table. "Is apple pie cooking in the oven, Mommy?" he asked. "Yes," answered his mother. "Hmmmm," said Robert as he stood on tiptoes and smelled a long, deep smell.

God made my nose so I can tell
What things are by the smell.

I smell apple pie!
I can tell
By the smell.

"Let's put onions in the salad," Mom said. Robert sat at the counter and watched his mother chop the onions. "Ooooh," Robert said, and he wrinkled his nose.

God made my nose so I can tell
What things are by the smell.

I smell onions!
I can tell
By the smell.

"Mommy, Mommy, I smell smoke!" yelled Robert. His mother ran to the oven and opened the oven door. "I think some juice from the apple pie spilled in the oven and burned," she explained. "But always get help when you smell smoke."

God made my nose so I can tell
What things are by the smell.

I smell smoke!
I can tell
By the smell.

9

"Do you need the clean socks sorted?" asked Robert. "That would be so helpful," his mother replied. Robert searched through the basket for all the socks. "Hmmmm," he said as he noticed the clean smell. Then he giggled. All of the socks were different colors. "At least they all smell nice and clean."

I could close my eyes, and still I'd know
If flowers in the garden grow.
I could close my eyes and without looking
Know an apple pie is cooking.
God has made my nose so I can tell.
Thank you, God, for the gift of smell.

10

**To Parents and Teachers**

*The Smells in God's World* is designed to help children grow in their appreciation for God's gift of smell. Children may also review colors and numbers and build vocabulary.

As you and your child enjoy reading *The Smells in God's World,* identify colors and numbers, name and count the colored objects, and name other parts of each picture. A prayer of thanksgiving may be appropriate.

Use of the audio cassette will enable children to repeat the story on their own.

Other titles in this series: *God Made the World We See, God's Gift of Touch, God Wants Us to Listen.*